# Engineers

Laura K. Murray

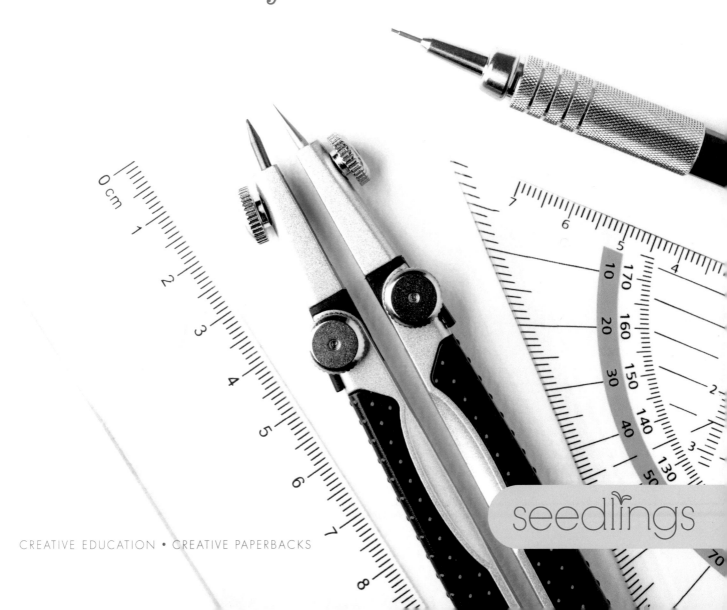

CREATIVE EDUCATION • CREATIVE PAPERBACKS

seedlings

Published by Creative Education and Creative Paperbacks
P.O. Box 227, Mankato, Minnesota 56002
Creative Education and Creative Paperbacks
are imprints of The Creative Company
www.thecreativecompany.us

Design by Ellen Huber
Production by Grant Gould
Art direction by Rita Marshall
Printed in the United States of America

Photographs by Alamy (dbimages, Stocksnapper, H. Mark
Weidman Photography), Getty (Jung Getty/Moment, Monty
Rakusen/Cultura, Ariel Skelley/DigitalVision), iStockphoto
(3DSculptor, andresr, Blade_kostas, BulentBARIS, Georgijevic,
gorodenkoff, grapix, rustemgurier, teekid, vm), Shutterstock
(Jenson, urfin)

ISBN 9781640264090 (library binding)
ISBN 9781628329421 (paperback)
ISBN 9781640005730 (eBook)

LCCN 2020907029

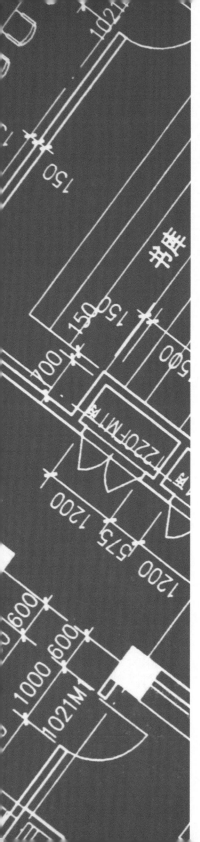
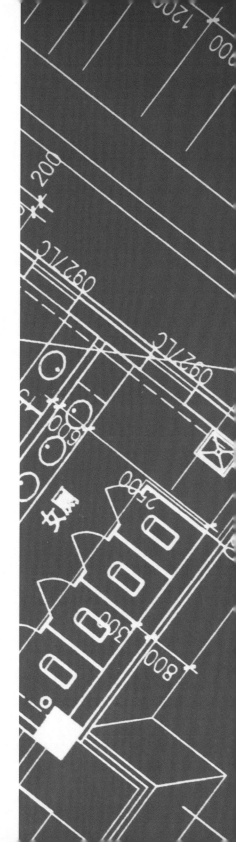

# TABLE OF CONTENTS

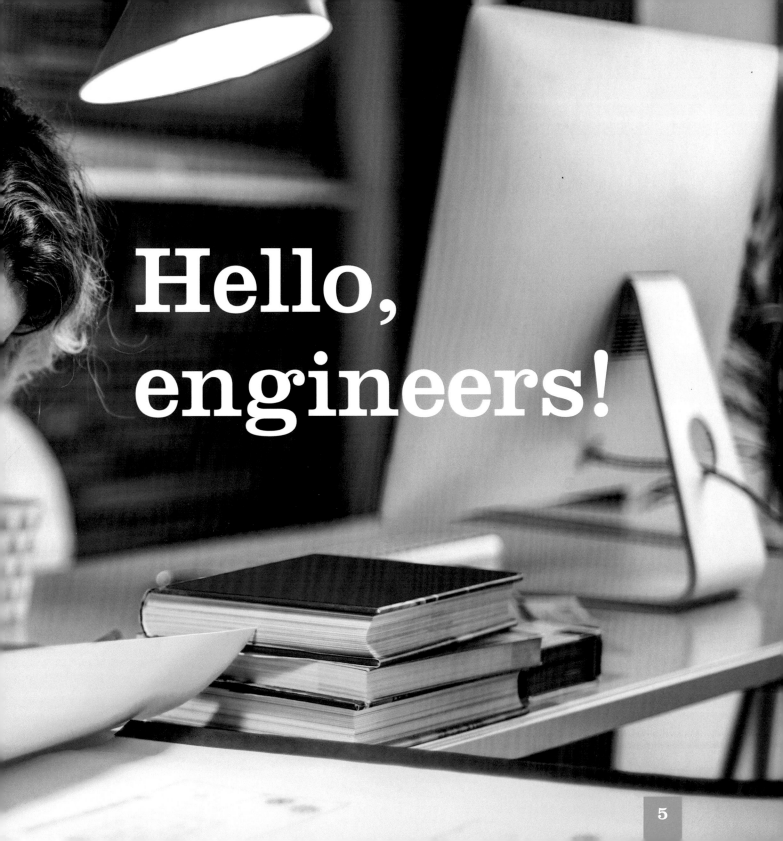

# Hello, engineers!

Engineers design and make new products. Some build roads and bridges.

Others make rockets.

# There are many kinds of engineers.

Some work in offices or labs.

Others work outside.

Some engineers help make cities.

They make sure homes have lights and water. They plan where the garbage will go.

Engineers make
buildings safe
from earthquakes.

They help keep
water and air clean.

Engineers use computers. They may work with big trucks or machines.

They use tools to find the size of things.

Engineers ask questions. They make plans.

They try out
their ideas.
They work to
solve problems.

# Thank you, engineers!

# Picture an Engineer

drafting triangle

blueprint

computer

hardhat

ruler

pen

## Words to Know

**earthquakes:** shaking of the ground

**labs:** places with special tools to test an idea to a problem

# Read More

Bowman, Chris. *Highways*.
Minneapolis: Bellwether Media, 2019.

Dittmer, Lori. *Golden Gate Bridge*.
Mankato, Minn.: Creative Education, 2020.

## Websites

Engineering for Kids
http://www.sciencekids.co.nz/engineering.html

**What is an Engineer?**
https://thekidshouldseethis.com/post/whats-an-engineer

# Index